SRA Reading Mastery

Signature Edition

Literature Guide
Grade 1

Siegfried Engelmann

McGraw Hill SRA

Columbus, OH

SRAonline.com

 SRA

Send all inquiries to this address:
SRA/McGraw-Hill
4400 Easton Commons
Columbus, OH 43219

ISBN: 978-0-07-612467-1
MHID: 0-07-612467-3

10 11 12 13 14 15 RHR 17 16 15 14

Contents

Reading Mastery, Grade 1
Literature Guide

INTRODUCTION

Nine literature selections are designed to accompany *Reading Mastery Signature Edition,* Grade 1. They elaborate on the skills the children are learning in *Reading Mastery,* provide children with a wider genre of literature than provided elsewhere in the program, and sharpen their understanding of story grammar, structure, and story morals developed in *Reading Mastery.*

Below is a list of the selections and an indication of the earliest *Reading Mastery* lesson after which each selection is to be presented.

LITERATURE SELECTIONS

Follows Lesson	Title	Author
5	*One Little Kitten*	Tana Hoban
15	*The Carrot Seed*	Ruth Krauss
20	*Who Took the Farmer's Hat?*	Joan L. Nõdset
25	*A Kiss for Little Bear*	Else Holmelund Minarik
30	*Molly's Bracelet*	Isabel Bissett
35	*There Stood Our Dog*	Anne Houghton
40	*Fat Cat Tompkin*	Diana Noonan
45	*In the Forest*	Stephen Ray and Kathleen Murdoch
50	*The Perfects*	Marjorie Weinman Sharmat

Story Summaries

One Little Kitten is a story about a kitten that discovers exciting places to play and hide. Photographs show the kitten's activities.

The Carrot Seed is a story about a boy who plants a carrot seed. Members of his family tell the boy that the seed will not grow. But it does grow—into a gigantic carrot.

Who Took the Farmer's Hat? tells how the wind carries a farmer's old brown hat on a journey that ends when the hat becomes a bird's nest. The farmer follows the hat, but when he sees that it is being used as a nest, he decides to buy a new brown hat.

A Kiss for Little Bear is a humorous story in which a grandmother bear receives a picture Little Bear has made for her. She sends a kiss to him by pony express—through several animals—and the kiss almost gets lost.

Molly's Bracelet tells about Molly's search for the gold bracelet she lost. Months later she finds it in an apple tree. It is still shiny because it is gold.

There Stood Our Dog is a story about a dog that mysteriously escapes from a yard that has a high fence, locked gates, and no holes. The dog's family spies on her and finally discovers that she uses the trampoline to bounce her way out of the yard.

Fat Cat Tompkin is a humorous story about Miss Pots's mean and large cat, Tompkin, who must go to the vet every month. It takes great effort to catch the cat and transport him, but he gets an A for good health.

In the Forest is a story about a hungry lizard that lives in the forest and tries unsuccessfully to catch a spider.

The Perfects is a story about a perfect family that is frustrated by trying to find a perfect spot for a perfect picnic. The Perfects learn the lesson that there's more than one way to be perfect (like perfectly messy).

Presenting the Books

The selections are keyed to the reading vocabulary that children are learning in *Reading Mastery*, Grade 1. The earlier stories involve simpler vocabulary and the later stories present more sophisticated words. The stories also increase in length. Each selection has some words that have not yet been taught in *Reading Mastery*. This guide specifies these words and provides directions for teaching them before the children read the story in a small group.

The literature selections present a variety of book styles. Some are classics *(The Carrot Seed, Who Took the Farmer's Hat?)*, some are modern *(Molly's Bracelet, There Stood Our Dog)*, and some present engaging pictures *(One Little Kitten, In the Forest)*. All present text that the children will be able to read, and all are enjoyable.

The literature selections are valuable additions to the regular *Reading Mastery* lessons for several reasons. They help provide a transition from the kind of print that is in the early part of Grade 1 to regular print. They broaden the scope of literacy experiences the children have and acquaint children with story formats different from those in *Reading Mastery*. Most importantly, they present selections that do not diminish in impact when they are reread.

The suggested schedule for the literature activities follows. The schedule provides for work with the literature selections every fifth lesson, starting with lesson 5.

SCHEDULE OF LITERATURE SELECTIONS

Reading Mastery Lesson	5	10	15	20	25	30	35	40	45	50	55	60	65	70	75
Title															
One Little Kitten	A										B				
The Carrot Seed			A										B		
Who Took the Farmer's Hat?				A										B	
A Kiss for Little Bear					A										B
Molly's Bracelet						A									
There Stood Our Dog							A								
Fat Cat Tompkin								A							
In the Forest									A						
The Perfects										A					

The literature lessons involve three readings of each selection, labeled A, B, and C.

Reading A—Teacher Reading. This is a story reading by the teacher with emphasis on the sequence of events and details of the pictures presented in the selection. Children follow along in their books.

Reading B—Group Reading. First the children identify the new words that are in the selection. Then the teacher reads the selection as the children follow along. Finally the children read the selection. The B reading is designed so that children become familiar with the words that are presented in traditional orthography. (In the *Reading Mastery* lessons, children are still reading words that are prompted with joined letters and lines over some vowels. In the literature selections the words are in regular print.)

Reading C—Independent Reading. The C reading is an individual reading check-out. First children read the selection to the teacher and answer questions. Then they are permitted to take the selection home and read it to members of their family.

Reading Mastery Lesson	80	85	90	95	100	105	110	115	120	125	130	135	140	145	150
Title															
One Little Kitten						C									
The Carrot Seed								C							
Who Took the Farmer's Hat?									C						
A Kiss for Little Bear										C					
Molly's Bracelet	B										C				
There Stood Our Dog		B										C			
Fat Cat Tompkin			B										C		
In the Forest				B										C	
The Perfects					B										C

Materials. You will need enough copies of the books so that each child in a small reading group has a copy. No other special materials are needed.

Setup. Ideally, the books should **not** be presented as part of the regular reading lessons, but during a time when children do extensions or independent work, or before or after the reading lesson. Scheduling the literature lesson at a time that is removed from the reading period is preferable.

Introducing the program. (Tell the children:) We're going to read some library books. These books have regular type and nice pictures. I'll read the stories to you, then later in the year, you'll read the stories and get to take them home so you can read them to your family.

Reading A—Teacher Reading

The A readings begin on lesson 5 and continue through lesson 50. During this time, you will do an A reading with each selection. Follow these steps:

1. **Pass out books to children.** Tell them: Don't open the book yet. We will go through the book together. I'll tell you when to open the book and when to turn the page.

2. **Direct children to touch the words of the title as you read them.**

3. **Go through the story.** For each page:
   a. Refer to the picture and either ask about or point out relevant details.
   b. Read the text.
   c. Point out those details of the story that are important for comprehension. (These point-outs are listed in the literature lesson for each selection.)
   d. Direct children to go to the next page.

Example
One Little Kitten (first selection)

The title is on the cover in yellow print. Touch it. *One Little Kitten.* And who is that in the picture next to the title? Yes, that's the little kitten. Open the book to the first page that has a big picture of the kitten on it. Look closely at that picture. I think the kitten is licking something. What's that? *Its paw.*

- I'll read what it says on that page:
  A new day!
What time of day is it—early in the morning or late at night? *Early.*

- Yes, it's a new day.
  Touch the picture on the next page.
  What's the kitten doing in that picture? *Playing with the basket.*

- I'll read what it says:
  It's time to play.
  Turn to the next page. Where is the kitten now? *In the basket.*

- I'll read what it says:
  A place to hide.
  Where is the kitten hiding? *In a basket.*

---

   e. Repeat this basic procedure for each page.
   f. Maintain a good pace. Do not spend too much time on each page. Refer to each picture, read the text, and briefly relate the text back to the picture.

4. **Words and patterns.** After you go through the story the first time, identify some of the words the children can already read and those that are orthographically different from the word as it would appear in *Reading Mastery.* Also point out patterns. For example, tell the children: These words look different than they do in your reading program. Touch the last word on the first page of the story. That word is *day.* It doesn't have a line over the *a.* Touch the last word on the next page. That word doesn't have a line either. What's that word? *Play.*

- Yes, the parts of this book rhyme. Listen: A new *day.* It's time to *play.* The next two pages end with the words *hide* and *inside.* Those words rhyme.

5. **Children reading.** As a general rule, don't go through the entire selection a second time, but do a read-along with the first few pages. Let the children read the words that are familiar. For example, tell the children: You can read everything on the first two pages of this story. Call on a child to read the first page, or have the entire group read the first page.

6. **Additional activities.** Following the A reading of the selection, you may assign the children a variety of writing or drawing activities. Some suggestions appear with each literature selection. Following the reading of *One Little Kitten,* for example, you could make a cutout of a large basket and direct children to draw pictures of kittens doing different things. Children then cut out the pictures and put them in the basket. You could also have children copy a sentence from the story or the title of the story.

Summary of Reading A. The three major steps are:

    (1)   Read and interpret the story.
    (2)   Point out words and patterns.
    (3)   Repeat the first part of the selection with the children reading.

As children become familiar with the sequence of events, you may alter the presentation, but you should make sure that you refer to the pictures, read the text, point out patterns and words that are different than they appear in the *Reading Mastery* orthography, and provide some opportunity for the children to read parts of the selection.

Reading B—Group Reading

Reading B requires vocabulary preparation and a group reading of the entire selection. The B readings start on lesson 55 and continue through lesson 100. Children have already worked with each of the selections. Here are the steps for Reading B.

1. **Read new words.** Write the specified reading vocabulary words on the board. Model the reading of the words. Then direct children to read the words. For example, tell the children: The new words for *One Little Kitten* are *behind, broom, disappear, face, place, string, through, tight,* and *wait.* I'll read these words. Then you'll read them.

   Point to each word and read it. Then direct the children to read the words. Indicate the meaning of words that may be unfamiliar. For example, you could model *disappear.* When something disappears, you can't see it anymore. In the story we'll read, the kitten disappears.

2. **Read selection to children.** Read it all the way through one time, referring to the pictures as you did for Reading A. Then go through at least the first part of the selection a second time, with children pointing to the words as they are read.

   Do not read at a normal speaking rate, but at a rate that the children can maintain. You do not have to read every word. Direct the children to read some of the words, particularly those in the list they just read. For example, on rereading *One Little Kitten* tell the children: On this page, the kitten is going behind the broom. Follow along as I read. Is . . . there . . . Your turn: *Room.* Next page: Behind . . . this . . . Your turn: *Broom.*

3. **Direct children to read the entire selection.**
   Your turn to read the whole story.
   Call on individual children to read one or two parts of the text. Do not engage in a lot of comprehension activity on this reading. Praise children for accurate decoding, particularly the reading of the new words.

4. **Allow children access to the book following the reading.** Assign a time and place where children can study the book. Permit children who may be weak on the decoding of the story to study the story with a partner who reads well.

   Remind the children that they should try to read the whole story to themselves because that's what they'll do the next time the story is presented (Reading C). When they do a good job on this reading, they may take the book home and read it to their family.

   Selections 5, 6, and 9 are quite long and have more than ten new vocabulary words. The teaching of these words does not require as much practice as brand new words because the children have already been exposed to them during Reading A of the story. However, it may not be reasonable to present all the vocabulary and the reading of the story during the same period. A good plan for these selections is to present the work in two sessions. Present the first half of the vocabulary words and direct the reading and rereading of the first half of the selection. In the following session, present the second half of the vocabulary words and do the group reading for the second half of the story. Note: The literature lesson for some stories shows the vocabulary divided into more than one segment, and it shows the number of pages that are covered by each part of the vocabulary list.

Reading C—Independent Reading

Reading C involves a fast children's reread of the selection, followed by comprehension questions that children answer, either in writing or orally. Following successful performance on the C reading, children take the book home for a specified period of time—one or two days. There should be no need for a vocabulary review to prepare the children for this reading.

For example, tell the children: We're going to read the story *One Little Kitten* again. Then you can take it home and read it to your family.

Call on individual children to read significant parts of the story. For the shorter stories, you may call on only two or three children to read the entire story. To give the other children in the group a turn, repeat the reading of the selection.

After children have read the selection, present the questions that are specified in the C reading. Note: You may want to test the children on additional information, including vocabulary words.

Summary of Activities for Each Selection

For each selection, the literature lesson lists the following:

- **Point-Outs for Reading A**

- **Additional Activities for Reading A:**
  Sentences or phrases for children to write
  Suggestions for additional story-related activities

- **New Reading Vocabulary for Reading B**

- **Questions for Reading C**

One Little Kitten

Written and Photographed by Tana Hoban

One Little Kitten is a story about a kitten that discovers exciting places to play and hide. Photographs show the kitten's activities.

	Follows *Reading Mastery* Lesson
Reading A – Teacher Reading	5
Reading B – Group Reading	55
Reading C – Independent Reading	105

Reading A—Teacher Reading (See pages 10–11.)

1. (Pass out **storybooks.**)
2. Find the **title.** Touch each word as I read it: *One . . . Little . . . Kitten.*
3. (Read and interpret the story. Refer to the point-outs listed below as you read.)

   Point-Outs
   - Point out places the kitten likes to hide. (In baskets, under toys, in sacks, behind brooms.)
   - Point out what the kitten does with the paper bag. (Hides in it.)
   - Point out who hugs the kitten. (The mother cat.)
   - Point out who the kitten is with at the end of the story. (The mother cat and other kittens.)
4. (Point out words and patterns.)
   - Identify words the children can already read and point out how the words are orthographically different from the words as they appear in *Reading Mastery.*
   - Point out the words that rhyme at the end of facing pages.
5. Reread the first part of the selection with the children.
6. **Copying**
   - Write this sentence on the board and have the children copy it: Hug me tight.
7. **Additional Activities**
   - Make cutouts of kittens and objects named in the story (basket, broom, pillow, bag.) Have children place kitten cutouts in or behind the cutouts of objects.

Reading B—Group Reading (See page 12.)

1. **New Reading Vocabulary. (Present new reading vocabulary.)**
   a. (Write *words* on the board.)

   Words

   behind
   broom
   disappear
   face
   place
   string
   through
   tight
   wait

   b. These are new words that are in the story I'm going to read to you. (Point to each word and read it.)
   c. Your turn to read the words. (Point to each word. Direct the children to read it.)
   d. (Present definitions.)

   Definitions
   - (Point to the word.) What word? *Disappear.*
   - When something **disappears,** you can't see it anymore. The kitten in the story disappears.

2. (Read the selection all the way through, referring to the pictures as you did for Reading A.)
3. (Reread the story. Direct the children to read some of the words.)
4. (Direct children to read the entire selection.)
5. (Assign a time and place for children to study the books.)

Reading C—Independent Reading (See page 13.)

1. (Reread the story. Call on individual children to read significant parts of the story.)
2. I'm going to ask you questions. (After children reread the story, ask them comprehension questions about the story.)

   Questions
   - Name some places the kitten likes to hide. *In baskets, under toys, in sacks, behind brooms.*
   - What did the kitten do with the paper bag? *Hid in it.*
   - Who hugged the kitten? *The mother cat.*
   - Who was the kitten with at the end of the story? *The mother cat and other kittens.*
3. (Have the children take the books home to read to family members.)

The Carrot Seed

Written by Ruth Krauss
Illustrated by Crockett Johnson

The Carrot Seed is a story about a boy who plants a carrot seed. Members of his family tell the boy that the seed will not grow. But it does grow—into a gigantic carrot.

	Follows *Reading Mastery* Lesson
Reading A – Teacher Reading	15
Reading B – Group Reading	65
Reading C – Independent Reading	115

Reading A—Teacher Reading

1. (Pass out **storybooks.**)
2. (Present **title.**) *The Carrot Seed.*
3. (Read and interpret the story. Refer to the point-outs listed below as you read.)

   Point-Outs
   - Point out who didn't think the carrot seed would come up. (The mother, father, and big brother.)
   - Point out that what the brother said was not as polite as what the mother and father said. (It won't come up.)
   - Point out the things the boy did each day. (Pulled weeds and sprinkled water on the ground.)
   - Point out how the carrot that came up was different from ordinary carrots. (It came up faster, was much bigger, and was redder.)
4. (Point out words and patterns.)
   - Identify words the children can already read and point out how the words are orthographically different from the words as they appear in *Reading Mastery.*
   - Point out the repeated phrases in the story. "It won't come up" and ". . . nothing came up."
5. (Reread the first part of the selection with the children.)
6. **Copying**
   - (Write on the board:) **A carrot came up.**
7. **Additional Activities**
   - Make a poster that shows the growth of a carrot. The poster should be a cutaway that shows carrots underground and above ground. Children make carrots of different sizes. Arrange them from left to right, with the smallest carrot first.

Reading B—Group Reading

1. **New Reading Vocabulary**

   Words
   - afraid
   - around
   - carrot
   - ground
   - nothing
   - pulled
   - seeds
   - sprinkle
   - water
   - weeds

   Definitions
   - When you **sprinkle** something, you spray it gently with water; you don't dump water on it.

2. (Read the selection all the way through, referring to the pictures as you did for Reading A.)
3. (Reread the story.)
4. (Direct children to read the entire selection.)
5. (Assign a time and place for children to study the books.)

Reading C—Independent Reading

1. (Reread the story.)
2. (Ask comprehension questions about the story.)

   Questions
   - Who thought the carrot seed would come up? *The boy.*
   - Who didn't think it would come up? *The mother, father, and brother.*
   - What did the boy do every day to help the carrot seed grow? *Pulled weeds and sprinkled water on the ground.*
   - How was the carrot different from ordinary carrots? *It came up faster, was much bigger, and was redder.*

3. (Have the children take the books home to read to family members.)

Who Took the Farmer's Hat?

Written by Joan L. Nödset
Illustrated by Fritz Siebel

Who Took the Farmer's Hat? tells how the wind carries a farmer's old brown hat on a journey that ends when the hat becomes a bird's nest. The farmer follows the hat, but when he sees that it is being used as a nest, he decides to buy a new brown hat.

	Follows *Reading Mastery* Lesson
Reading A – Teacher Reading	20
Reading B – Group Reading	70
Reading C – Independent Reading	120

Reading A—Teacher Reading

1. (Pass out **storybooks.**)
2. (Present **title.**) *Who Took the Farmer's Hat?*
3. (Read and interpret the story. Refer to the point-outs listed below as you read.)
   Point-Outs
   - Point out why the duck thought the hat was a boat. (It was floating in the water.)
   - Point out why the bird thought the hat was a nest. (It was the size and shape of a nest.)
   - Point out why the farmer didn't take the hat from the bird. (It was now a nest with an egg in it.)
4. (Point out words and patterns.)
   - Identify words the children can already read and point out how the words are orthographically different from the words as they appear in *Reading Mastery.*
   - Point out the repeated phrases in the story. ". . . did you see my old brown hat?" "No, . . . I saw . . ."
5. (Reread the first part of the selection with the children.)
6. **Copying**
   - (Write on the board:) **Where is my hat?**
7. **Additional Activities**
   - Prepare the children for a hat parade. Use small paper sacks as hats. Children can use cutouts, crayons, and scissors to design their hats and visors. Following the hat construction, the children can stage a hat parade and others can vote on the hit of the hat parade.

Reading B—Group Reading

1. **New Reading Vocabulary**

   Words
   - farmer
   - flowerpot
   - nest
   - new
   - nice
   - squirrel
   - wind

2. (Read the selection all the way through, referring to the pictures as you did for Reading A.)
3. (Reread the story.)
4. (Direct children to read the entire selection.)
5. (Assign a time and place for children to study the books.)

Reading C—Independent Reading

1. (Reread the story.)
2. (Ask comprehension questions about the story.)

   Questions
   - Why did the farmer lose his hat? *The wind blew it away.*
   - Why did the duck think the hat was a boat? *It was floating in the water.*
   - Where did the farmer find the hat? *In the tree.*
   - What was in the hat? *An egg.*
   - Did the farmer tell the bird that it was his hat? *No.*
   - Why didn't the farmer take the hat from the bird? *It was now a nest with an egg in it.*
   - Does the farmer have a hat now? *Yes.*

3. (Have the children take the books home to read to family members.)

A Kiss for Little Bear

Written by Else Holmelund Minarik
Illustrated by Maurice Sendak

A Kiss for Little Bear is a humorous story in which a grandmother bear receives a picture Little Bear has made for her. She sends a kiss to him by pony express—through several animals—and the kiss almost gets lost.

	Follows *Reading Mastery* Lesson
Reading A – Teacher Reading	25
Reading B – Group Reading	75
Reading C – Independent Reading	125

Reading A—Teacher Reading

1. (Pass out **storybooks.**)
2. (Present **title.**) *A Kiss for Little Bear.*
3. (Read and interpret the story. Refer to the point-outs listed below as you read.)

   Point-Outs
   - Point out what Little Bear made for his grandmother. (A picture.)
   - Point out who took the picture to the grandmother. (Hen.)
   - Point out who the frog gave the kiss to. (Cat.)
   - Point out who finally gave the kiss to Little Bear. (Hen.)
4. (Point out words and patterns.)
   - Identify words the children can already read and point out how the words are orthographically different from the words as they appear in *Reading Mastery.*
   - Point out the repeated phrases in the story. "I have a kiss for Little Bear." "It is from his grandmother."
5. (Reread the first part of the selection with the children.)
6. **Copying**
   - (Write on the board:) **The bear made a picture.**
7. **Additional Activities**
   - Make a poster with different animals carrying kisses. Cut out lips for the kisses. Have children draw different animals, including a picture of the grandmother bear. Arrange the animals so Hen is carrying the kiss back to Little Bear.

Reading B—Group Reading

1. **New Reading Vocabulary**

   Words

   decide

   grandmother

   Hen

   picture

   skunk

   wedding

   Definitions
   - When you **decide** to do something, you make up your mind to do it.

2. (Read the selection all the way through, referring to the pictures as you did for Reading A.)
3. (Reread the story.)
4. (Direct children to read the entire selection.)
5. (Assign a time and place for children to study the books.)

Reading C—Independent Reading

1. (Reread the story.)
2. (Ask comprehension questions about the story.)

   Questions
   - What did Little Bear make for somebody? *A picture.*
   - Who did he make it for? *Grandmother.*
   - Who took it to the grandmother? *Hen.*
   - What did Grandmother send back to Little Bear? *A kiss.*
   - Who did Grandmother give it to? *Hen.*
   - Who did Hen give it to? *Frog.*
   - Who did the frog give the kiss to? *Cat.*
   - Who finally gave the kiss to Little Bear? *Hen.*

3. (Have the children take the books home to read to family members.)

Molly's Bracelet

Written by Isabel Bissett
Illustrated by Heather Macallan

Molly's Bracelet tells about Molly's search for the gold bracelet she lost. Months later she finds it in an apple tree. It is still shiny because it is gold.

	Follows *Reading Mastery* Lesson
Reading A – Teacher Reading	30
Reading B – Group Reading	80
Reading C – Independent Reading	130

Reading A—Teacher Reading

1. (Pass out **storybooks**.)
2. (Present **title**.) *Molly's Bracelet.*
3. (Read and interpret the story. Refer to the point-outs listed below as you read.)

   ### Point-Outs
   Part 1: pages 2–16
   - Point out that the bracelet was made of real gold and must have cost a lot of money.
   - Point out where Molly lived. (On a farm.)
   - Point out where Molly was when she realized that she lost her bracelet. (In the bathtub.)
   - Point out that they didn't look in all the places Molly had been. (They didn't look in the tree.)
   - Point out the only time Molly sometimes felt sad. (At night, before falling asleep.)

   Part 2: pages 18–24
   - Point out the things she did in the summer and in the fall. (Swam, fished, made a flower garden, made a haystack, laid under an apple tree, looked for empty nests, looked for mushrooms, picked blackberries, picked apples.)
   - Point out that the apple tree had lots of leaves.
   - Point out what season it was when she finally found her bracelet. (Winter.)

4. (Point out words and patterns.)
   - Identify words the children can already read and point out how the words are orthographically different from the words as they appear in *Reading Mastery.*
   - Point out the repeated phrases in the story. "She wore it when. . . ." and "They looked. . . ."

5. (Reread the first part of the selection with the children.)

6. **Copying**
   - (Write on the board:) **She had a new bracelet.**
7. **Additional Activities**
   - Make bracelets. Cut aluminum wrap into long strips. Each child can fold and fashion the strip to make a bracelet. Have a bracelet parade.

Reading B—Group Reading

1. **New Reading Vocabulary**

   Words

   Part 1: pages 2–16
   bare
   bracelet
   except
   hopscotch
   lambs
   paddock
   swing
   wore

   Definitions
   - A **bracelet** is a piece of jewelry. Where do you wear a bracelet?
   - **Hopscotch** is a game that you play on a sidewalk. Who knows how to play it?
   - A **paddock** is a small, fenced-in area where animals stay.

   Part 2: pages 18–24
   blackberries
   garden
   haystack
   knitted
   mushrooms
   puddles
   ripe
   shiny
   snowy

2. (Read the selection all the way through, referring to the pictures as you did for Reading A.)
3. (Reread the story.)
4. (Direct children to reread the entire selection.)
5. (Assign a time and place for children to study the books.)

Reading C—Independent Reading

1. (Reread the story.)
2. (Ask comprehension questions about the story.)

   Questions
   - What gift did her father give her? *A gold bracelet.*
   - What was the bracelet made of? *Real gold.*
   - Where was Molly when she found out that she didn't have her bracelet? *In the bathtub.*
   - Where did she look? *Yard, paddock, path, by the swing.*
   - After a while, she didn't feel bad about the bracelet except at one time. When was that? *At night.*
   - What season was it when she finally found her bracelet? *Winter.*
   - Where was it? *In the apple tree.*
   - Why was it still shiny? *It was real gold.*

3. (Have the children take the books home to read to family members.)

There Stood Our Dog

Written by Anne Houghton
Illustrated by Craig Smith

There Stood Our Dog is a story about a dog that mysteriously escapes from a yard that has a high fence, locked gates, and no holes. The dog's family spies on her and finally discovers that she uses the trampoline to bounce her way out of the yard.

	Follows *Reading Mastery* Lesson
Reading A – Teacher Reading	35
Reading B – Group Reading	85
Reading C – Independent Reading	135

Reading A—Teacher Reading

1. (Pass out **storybooks.**)
2. (Present **title.**) *There Stood Our Dog.*
3. (Read and interpret the story. Refer to the point-outs listed below as you read.)

   Point-Outs
   Part 1: pages 2–8
   - Point out who is standing at the front door. (The dog.)
   - Point out the fences and the gates around the backyard.
   - Point out who is standing outside the school. (The dog.)
   - Point out who is standing outside the store. (The dog.)
   - Point out who is standing next to the neighbor. (The dog.)

   Part 2: Pages 9–16
   - Point out where the sister is hiding. (Behind a tree.)
   - Point out where Dad is hiding. (In the shed.)
   - Point out where Mom is hiding. (In the playhouse.)
   - Point out what the dog is doing. (Bouncing on the trampoline.)
   - Point out what the family is doing. (Moving the trampoline.)

4. (Point out words and patterns.)
   - Identify words the children can already read and point out how the words are orthographically different from the words as they appear in *Reading Mastery*.
   - Point out the repeated phrases in the story. ". . . there stood our dog. How did she get out?" "We checked the fences. There were no holes. We checked the gates. They were locked."

5. (Reread the first part of the selection with the children.)
6. **Copying**
    • (Write on the board:) **How did she get out?**
7. **Additional Activities**
    • Make a model of a trampoline. Tie rubber bands to the four corners of a washcloth or rectangular rag. Connect the rubber bands to stationary objects. Drop small objects on the trampoline. They will bounce.

Reading B—Group Reading

1. **New Reading Vocabulary**
    Words
    Part 1: pages 1–8
      backyard
      brought
      checked
      doorbell
      fences
      locked
      neighbor
      Tuesday
      Wednesday
    Part 2: pages 9–16
      binoculars
      bounce
      kennel
      leapt
      playhouse
      roof
      springs
      trampoline

    Definitions
    • When you look through **binoculars,** things look like they are much closer than they really are.
    • A **kennel** is a kind of doghouse.
2. (Read the selection all the way through, referring to the pictures as you did for Reading A.)
3. (Reread the story.)
4. (Direct children to read the entire selection.)
5. (Assign a time and place for children to study the books.)

Reading C—Independent Reading

1. (Reread the story.)
2. (Ask comprehension questions about the story.)

   ### Questions
   - Who kept getting out of the yard? *The dog.*
   - What did the family check every time they found out the dog had escaped? *Fences, gates.*
   - Name some places they would find the dog. *At the front door, at school, at the store.*
   - What was the first day they watched the dog? *Saturday.*
   - Where did the person who is telling the story hide to watch the dog? *On the shed roof.*
   - On which day did they find out how the dog got out? *Sunday.*
   - What did the dog do to get out? *Leapt up and down on the trampoline.*
   - What did the family do to make sure the dog couldn't do that anymore? *Moved the trampoline.*

3. (Have the children take the books home to read to family members.)

Fat Cat Tompkin

Written by Diana Noonan
Illustrated by Craig Smith

Fat Cat Tompkin is a humorous story about Miss Pots's mean and large cat, Tompkin, who must go to the vet every month. It takes great effort to catch the cat and transport him, but he gets an A for good health.

	Follows *Reading Mastery* Lesson
Reading A – Teacher Reading	40
Reading B – Group Reading	90
Reading C – Independent Reading	140

Reading A—Teacher Reading

1. (Pass out **storybooks.**)
2. (Present **title.**) *Fat Cat Tompkin.*
3. (Read and interpret the story. Refer to the point-out listed below as you read.)

   Point-Outs
   * When Tompkin gets an A in health, it means that he is in very good health.
4. (Point out words and patterns.)
   * Identify words the children can already read and point out how the words are orthographically different from the words as they appear in *Reading Mastery.*
   * Read sentences from the story, omitting the last word. Have the children use picture clues to complete the sentences.
5. (Reread the first part of the selection with the children.)
6. **Copying**
   * (Write on the board:) **Tompkin is a fat cat.**
7. **Additional Activities**
   * Make certificates for pets. Each certificate shows a picture of the pet and reads: My pet gets an A.

Reading B—Group Reading

1. **New Reading Vocabulary**

   Words
   - catch
   - certificate
   - health
   - month
   - share
   - sure
   - terrified
   - Tompkin

2. (Read the selection all the way through, referring to the pictures as you did for Reading A.)
3. (Reread the story.)
4. (Direct children to read the entire selection.)
5. (Assign a time and place for children to study the books.)

Reading C—Independent Reading

1. (Reread the story.)
2. (Ask comprehension questions about the story.)

   Questions
   - Who owns Tompkin? *Miss Pots.*
   - How big is Tompkin? *Very big.*
   - How do the other cats feel about him? *They're terrified of him.*
   - Where do they have to take Tompkin every month? *To the vet.*
   - Where does he try to hide? *Under the bed.*
   - What does her dad say he is? *A lion.*
   - Why can't he get through the open window? *He's too fat.*
   - Why doesn't he fit in his cat box? *He's too fat.*
   - Is Tompkin in bad health or good health? *Good health.*
   - They say that they don't mind helping Miss Pots next time. Do you think they're telling the truth? *No.*

3. (Have the children take the books home to read to family members.)

LITERATURE LESSON 8
In the Forest

Written by Stephen Ray and Kathleen Murdoch
Illustrated by Trevor Ruth

In the Forest is a story about a hungry lizard that lives in the forest and tries unsuccessfully to catch a spider.

	Follows *Reading Mastery* Lesson
Reading A – Teacher Reading	45
Reading B – Group Reading	95
Reading C – Independent Reading	145

Reading A—Teacher Reading

1. (Pass out **storybooks.**)
2. (Present **title.**) *In the Forest.*
3. (Read and interpret the story. Refer to the point-out listed below as you read.)

   Point-Outs
   - Point out what the spider did to get away from the lizard. (Dropped down the tree on some spinning silk.)
4. (Point out words and patterns.)
   - Identify words the children can already read and point out how the words are orthographically different from the words as they appear in *Reading Mastery.*
   - Point out that this is a cumulative story.
5. (Reread the first part of the selection with the children.)
6. **Copying**
   - (Write on the board:) **The tree had a twisting branch.**
7. **Additional Activities**
   - Make spiders. Provide each child with a round paper circle and eight narrow strips of paper. Children make one accordion fold in each strip. The strips are now legs that may be pasted onto the circle. Children then decorate the circle with eyes and designs.

Reading B—Group Reading

1. **New Reading Vocabulary**

   Words

   flaky

   hollow

   lizard

   lumpy

   spider

   twisting

2. (Read the selection all the way through, referring to the pictures as you did for Reading A.)
3. (Reread the story.)
4. (Direct children to read the entire selection.)
5. (Assign a time and place for children to study the books.)

Reading C—Independent Reading

1. (Reread the story.)
2. (Ask comprehension questions about the story.)

   Questions

   - Where was the tree? *In the forest.*
   - Name two things that were inside the hollow. *Leaves, a lizard.*
   - What was near the lizard? *A spider.*
   - What did the lizard want to do with that spider? *Eat it.*
   - Did tho lizard havo good luck or bad luck? *Bad.*
   - Why was his luck bad? *The spider got away.*

3. (Have the children take the books home to read to family members.)

The Perfects

Written by Marjorie Weinman Sharmat
Illustrated by Mark Corcoran

The Perfects is a story about a perfect family that is frustrated by trying to find a perfect spot for a perfect picnic. The Perfects learn the lesson that there's more than one way to be perfect (like perfectly messy).

	Follows *Reading Mastery* Lesson
Reading A – Teacher Reading	50
Reading B – Group Reading	100
Reading C – Independent Reading	150

Reading A—Teacher Reading

1. (Pass out **storybooks.**)
2. (Present **title.**) *The Perfects.*
3. (Read and interpret the story. Refer to the point-outs listed below as you read.)
   Point-Outs
   Part 1: pages 2–6
   - Point out Mr. and Mrs. Perfect.
   - Point out Fritz and Dudley Perfect and the dogs, Fritz and Dudley.
   - Point out the perfect bedroom.
   - Point out the characters walking to the woods. (Mr. and Mrs. Perfect, Fritz and Dudley Perfect, and the dogs, Fritz and Dudley.)

   Part 2: pages 7–16
   - Point out the features of the first place they chose to have a picnic. (On a bench with splinters, under a tree that is dropping its leaves, near a brook with a strange gurgle.)
   - Point out what Fritz is doing. (Jumping in the air because he sat on a sharp rock.)
   - Point out what the Perfects are running from. (Bees.)
   - Point out where the Perfects decide to have their picnic. (At the top of a hill.)
   - Point out what happened to the Perfects when they climbed the hill. (They slid backward down the hill and landed in a heap at the bottom.)
   - Point out how the Perfects looked after they fell down the hill. (Their clothes were ripped and their hair was tangled.)
   - Point out where the Perfects finally ate their picnic lunch. (At the first place—on the bench with splinters, under the tree with the falling leaves, near the brook.)

4. (Point out words and patterns.)
   - Identify words the children can already read and point out how the words are orthographically different from the words as they appear in *Reading Mastery.*
5. (Reread the first part of the selection with the children.)
6. **Copying**
   - (Write on the board:) **The Perfects packed a perfect lunch.**
7. **Additional Activities**
   - Make pictures of the Perfects before and after the picnic. Trace the pictures of the Perfects on page 6. Give copies to the children and have them modify the picture to show how the Perfects looked at the end of the story.

Reading B—Group Reading

1. **New Reading Vocabulary**

   Words
   Part 1: pages 1–7
   aren't
   bench
   brook
   doesn't
   flies
   gurgle
   Mrs.
   parent
   perfect
   picnic
   sense
   sons
   splinters
   thought

   Definitions
   - **Aren't** means "are not." If you aren't happy, you are not happy.
   - A **brook** is a small stream.
   - **Doesn't** means "does not." If she doesn't eat, she does not eat.
   - If something makes good **sense,** it is a good idea.
   - **Splinters** are small, sharp pieces of wood that can get under your skin and hurt a lot.

Part 2: pages 8–16

awful
backward
climb
family
high
hour
huffed
messy
ouch
pointed
possible
quite
ripped
sandwiches
stretched
stupid

Definitions

- If something is **possible,** it could happen. If something is not possible, it can't happen.

2. (Read the selection all the way through, referring to the pictures as you did for Reading A.)
3. (Reread the story.)
4. (Direct children to read the entire selection.)
5. (Assign a time and place for children to study the books.)

Reading C—Independent Reading

1. (Reread the story.)
2. (Ask comprehension questions about the story.)
   Questions
   - Name things that are perfect about the Perfect family. *Their teeth, hair, clothes, sons, and dogs.*
   - What were the sons named? *Fritz and Dudley.*
   - What were the dogs named? *Fritz and Dudley.*
   - Where did they go to have their perfect picnic? *To the woods.*
   - What didn't the Perfects like about the bench that was under the tree near the brook? *It had splinters.*
   - Who found a place that seemed perfect? *Mrs. Perfect.*
   - Why did they run from that place? *Bees.*

- How long did the Perfects climb the hill? *One hour.*
- Who slid down the hill first? *Mrs. Perfect.*
- What happened to the rest of the Perfects? *They started to slide.*
- What did Dudley and Fritz say picnics were for? *Eating, stuffing yourself, getting messy and dirty, and having fun.*
- Where did the Perfects finally go for their picnic? *To the bench under the tree near the brook.*
- What was perfect about the Perfects at the end of the story? *They were perfectly stuffed, perfectly messy, and perfectly happy.*

3. (Have the children take the books home to read to family members.)